LIVING IN THIS SKIN

(BLACK BRITISH POETRY)

ISBN: 978 1 79299 193 6

Published by Martin Rumble

www.facebook.com/martin.rumble8

Here is a collection of lyrics covering the trials of friendship, the Black experience, Black fatherhood and a deep mathematical understanding of God. These are the poetic expressions of experiences and observations from a Pan-African's perspective.

Martin Rumble

<u>LIVING IN THIS SKIN</u>

CONTENTS

Family

When I was lost in a backwards life
I made a vow to God and my future wife
To unite and strive
        To only put constant people in our seed's life
We see our seeds as precious
        And to prepare them for a harsh world, we take every measure
I want my seeds to grow up with secure roots
  Where family is their support group, who are really for you
    That sees them more than an obligation
      Who makes time for special occasions
        Like they were special relations
I solemnly refuse to have my kids grow up confused
  Or pampered
    So, we will be their anchors
      So, they don't become selfish adults walking backwards
Too many kids grow up in tatters, with no manners
  So, it's paramount to us that they realise that they matter

I want real loved ones in their life and not actors
  There's no playing a part; show love then disregard
    It has to be coming straight from the heart

My ways may seem different
  But I've got the best intentions
    It's just that my beliefs are not bending
      And I believe that family should not just be seen at births, funerals and weddings
     Yet my hand is always extending
      Until there's tension
       And when it comes to the seeds, I cause no intervention
      Unless their pain I'm preventing
      I have my flaws and put up walls
       But I'd sacrifice it all because for the seeds it's all for

We open doors for the consistent and thoughtful
  And close doors forceful
    On those behaving like they've picken the short straw

They're not always a pleasure
  But never a chore
    As we make the blueprint for when their children fall
We raise them with manners and respect
  And to overstand what LOVE is
    So that they can see when others put selfishness above this

Some kids naturally have so much love to give
  But when there's a chance to return their love
    They keep getting put to the back of the list
      And thoughtlessly missed
        Because so many people are about ME and Mine and never find the time
Don't they know that love is shown at the most inconvenient of times
  And its definition lies in self-sacrifice.

The Headmaster

A manipulator in charge, with false charm, holding all the cards

Rather than employ good teachers, he'd prefer to put money onto his car

What kind of parents are we, putting our seeds in the hands of a tyrant?

His ego needs good teachers to admire him

But it's hard when money is the basis of his hiring and firing

Authoritarian

      Camouflaged barbarian, got our children fearing him

         A totalitarian

            Walking corridors as if his way is flawless

With a way deeply lawless

      Hiding behind our babies and his teachers' skirts

How can he know a man's worth

      -When he gets women to carry out his filthy work?

User, with all your props it must be hard to see the reflection of a LOSER

      A snake in a suit running your children's school

Senior staff representing a fool, they're lifeless, only existing to be used as his TOOL

      Paying a price priceless

He's resting his dirty feet on you, complacent pedestals

      When he eventually topples

         They'd be no green bottles

            After the foundation of the school wobbles

This inhumane vampire, like leaches sucking the GOD given light

            Out of the souls of these innocent teachers

      Then hanging them out to dry and not man enough to look them in the eye

         When dismissing them with his lies and pretence that's

-coated with an insensitivity immense

            All whilst sucking on his cancer stick of false confidence

Does the man have no conscience?

      Your name is notoriously known

         Your way is the Devil's own

         Your fate is engraved in stone

What are you gonna do when all that's left is to reflect in retirement

And your control is taken away from your environment

All because you weren't achieving what you're needing
    But instead reaching for all that you're desiring

This is a warning a calling to all parents
    When choosing a school look beyond its appearance
      And look for what's realistic that surpasses statistics
    The well-being of our children we can't risk it
Don't get complacent or leave it too late to fix it
    Research and take a vested interest in the school's head
      What does he stand for?
        What are his rules?
          Your seeds are special you must take time to choose
            Their schools
Because the school is only an extension of his views
    If an insensitive silver spooned bandit
      Can take his good teachers for more than granted
Then it's guaranteed that your children are not to be inspired but are to be managed
        In the hands of a money motivated savage
If he is moral-less how can he see to encourage high principles in the youth?
No matter what the IQ
    Without good values
      Our children become intelligent fools
Good teachers you must face this
    Your good energy is worth more than a payslip
    Please don't waste it, rowing to the beat in support of the headmaster's slaveship
For every ten bad places
    Around the corner there is always something more worthwhile waiting
    God works in mysterious ways and only guides the steadfast and patient

Black Holocaust

Have a spoonful of true reality
　　　Let you think twice before you go back to your physical fantasy
　　　　Concerning slavery,
　　　　　Some say get over it
　　　　　　But that's no solution
When slave traders got over it with the industrial revolution
　　　Racism wasn't created by racists
　　　　But by economists
　　　　　A sour concept was sold
　　　　That the masses accepted to lighten their load
　　　Causing all manner of atrocities for power
Cut off a race castrated and deflowered
　　　Now we self-destructively devour
I'm not bitter cus I'm bitter
　　　I'm bitter cus your way remains
　　　　　Same face but masked with the illusion of sincerity and grace

With the blood of those enslaved running through my veins
How can you get over what's rubbed in your face?
　　　In a place I was self-raised
　　　　　And Edward Colston's statue still remains, still stands
The man who made a living from shipping
　　　　　　　In cramped conditions
　　　　　Unwilling men, women and children
So they can live a life of cotton picking, to have his pockets filling
　　　Where's the conscience God given?
His polished image represents present day's state of racism and ignorance
　　　　　　　　It's sickening
And the media are still subliminally hitting
　　　　And I refuse to be pacified into submission
　　　　　　　　And pigeon-holed into position
　　　Like 2Pac said "This ain't living"
When you're governed by pompous half-wits

I can see why ignorance is bliss

When you're knee deep in this wishy-washyness

Where the Prejudist hide behind political correctness

But wisdom and understanding encourages seeking and finding

And keeps reminding me of the shackles and chains

And the European economy built off the backs of slaves, where I came

And only true success can break the stale mate

And I'm shouting for change and I know <u>initially</u> it was never a race thing

It was a money make thing

And nothing has changed

There are just different ways for power to be obtained

So Much More

I'm not having it
>>> Blacks, more than mindless thugs and sexual savages

Blacks, mentally endowed
>>> As we spiritually prowl

Part of a higher civilisation
>>> Which left behind a state of mind that we can still be obtaining
>>>> Even in an environment full of racism
>>>>> That we were made slaves in
>>>>>> And our minds were raised in
>>>>>>> Where most of us have complexes of identification
>>>>> Where the only way up is to be the court jester
>>> Or washed western

As Uncle Toms aspire to be the exception
>>> Whilst Black history is still going unmentioned
>>>> And racists are still growing with ill intention
>>>>> I'm sick-a-dem

This racist government should put Black history into the school curriculum
>>> As the educational system only briefly mentions
>>>> And then wonders why the narrow minded of those white
>>>>>> Don't have an understanding of acceptance

As we're imprisoned or sectioned
>>> And conditioned to self-hate as we find each other detesting

I'm telling them
>>> To forget trying to lighten our complexion
>>>> And make us become more western
>>>>> When we should be treasuring our melanin
>>> And take things back to the source

Yes, we've become rebels
>>> And our cause,
>>>> Is that we derive from a people who followed ancient laws

That date way before the Bible was formed

As we're kept lost cus racist historians are at odds

When they see us depicted on ancient walls as kings, queens and gods

As around their collars they're getting hot

But in western racist history books we're still getting forgot

This is a different time, a different era

Where a man's complexion is still his terror

Instead of a complete pleasure

As the media might as well take every measure

To straighten, demean and make Black better

With racist tremors

As I verbally make clear the dilemma

Black history has been hidden in a frustrated temper

And they're showing no retreat, no surrender

When it should be shoved in the face to educate

Slavery made a derogatory distinction in race

That discriminates the Black face

That has echoed to present day

All I do is put things back in their rightful place

So, I must first differentiate

This country was built off the backs of a high-cultured race

Reduced to being seen as sub-human slaves

In the stroke of a pen, by the minds of mad men

And a whole nation backed them

And now they prefer to fear me, than hear me

And the depth of the rabbit hole may seem scary

But we're tracing back and digging up the truths buried

Cus it's too late to hide the painted walls in the pyramids of Ta-Merry

Beyond an Opinion

All praises to the most high for encouraging me to listen
And making me a man of wisdom
Enabling me to see beyond my many defence mechanisms
That had me selfishly existing

I was intelligently stupid
Lived a life behind selfish excuses
Which makes it harder to see where the universal truth is

Which goes beyond a person's opinion
Where only those who know truth, know its weight because they're living it
This gift, for those I have love for, I'm giving it

Where's the sense?
When so many unite in their weaknesses and not their strengths
You see, this western system encourages division
Wanting us to think everybody's different
So, we are unified only in a divisive dominion
But when truth is spoken it obliterates opinion

Truth is spoken at a time of harvest
It hits those puffed with pride the harshest
Truth offends
When you talk the harsh truth, you lose friends
Because their only choices are admittance or pretence

I'm impelled to talk truth
Because it's the only defence against a world where egos are overwhelmed by 'yes' men
Whilst pride prevents them from self-reinventing
And resurrecting
Higher desires of self-bettering

Only holla if your hearts have heard me

-You see, the truth isn't a selfish journey

It's your empathy for others that depicts if you're worthy

How much water you'd give a dying man if you were really thirsty

Don't you see, to agree to disagree to a universal truth has serious ramifications

It means one of us is going against creation

There is no easy way to say this

When you're in a selfish way of thinking, you are being complacent

    This means,

        In man's weak image,

            Your minds are shaped, moulded and created

                As you become just another pod plugged into the Matrix

The Rebuke

I forever observe the rule
> That people will do what you allow them to
>> But when you attempt to deceive someone honest, for your own gain
>> You are the one who eventually deals with the pain

I've been through it
> Lived a life intelligently stupid

Now raised from the death of a foul youth
> By constant self-rebuking
>> Cus old habits are constantly pursuing

> For years, I've been calming my inner thug

And every written prayer brings me closer to the innocence of doves
> Keeping everything worthwhile as 'one'

True prayer is like a reset
> All the built-up pride and jealousy and this worldly world's effect is put to death
>> In a moment of clarity
>>> Where man is not living for his own vanity
>>> But is blessed with a new visibility
>>> Not eluded by false imagery
>>>> As it brings you back to your natural state of
>>>>> HUMILITY
>>>> Which is *really living.*
>>>>> Without God, we're only existing

This corpse of a world that I was once embracing
> I am now hating
>> I now live for the giving
>>> When most live for the taking

Between good friends God is mediating
> So, I will never move with someone through obligation

-I'm either feeling you or I'm feeling the presence of SATAN

Heavy garbs of self-illusion conceal the naked

But to those who don't fake it, a fool's way is obvious and blatant

So, friendships are formed through a patience that leads to a deep trust

Cus halfway friends, with no sense, take kindness for weakness

As their judgements, ill-informed assumptions, has me

SPEECHLESS

So that I won't be disappointed by fools

I try to overcome my problem of giving credit where it is not due

That is why this wake-up alarm is dedicated to

All those who

Are in the pursuit of TRUTH

Gold Dust

These words are gold dust

To those struggling in an ignorance vigorous

Incarcerated in a mental slavery veiled cus so hideous

By lower-self prevailed idiots derailing nations

I'm just articulating the despicable acts of those ordained by Satan

        Those conscience aching religious atheists

        Crusading whilst causing a humiliation that's proliferating throughout creation

          To know thy self

        Is the only retaliation

That exposes the root of the HUMILIATION

        That stops higher-self awakening with lower-self praising

           In a materialistic world that hell's raising

Where the majority are potential agents, stuck to their sticky cravings

        Caught in a time signless

          When time has no patience for human kindness

                If you're trying to make it

      And you'd never find your way out of the matrix

Cus there's no self-saviour

      When self-preservation comes before your neighbour

This is my duty

      That my conscience pursues and the false ambition of man, manifested, eludes

These words

      These lyrics

        This verse

          With all I'm worth, I SERVE

I do it for mankind but at the same time, I wouldn't put it after any man on earth

What helps me refrain from evil is remembering

      That all men are created with the potential to be equal

           And it's your humility that makes you regal

        And the material is immaterial and sacrificing it gives you imperial eyes

In this selfish self-inflicted life, it's not enough to just be kind if you're blind

      Unforeseen problems materialise right before your eyes

           Like magic

-Cus you didn't check yourself, you missed the warning signs

Of the Source's mathematics

The wise are imperial and regal in action, born from sight

Only gained through self-sacrifice of selfishness and pride,

Where the devil's seven steps behind,

And no material possessions or desires have them tied

Behind this lust is where fools hide

So, I remind them with lyrics that ignite an inner self-sight

That encourages man not to be stagnant

Where he's in fragments

So, he can pull himself together with self-prevailing actions

Stars That ~~Can't~~ Won't Sparkle

I thought my close shave would kick start

My close stars into action

But as quickly as they awoke

They went back to their distractions

Self-absorbing

Why live a selfish life of YOU AND YOURS?

When US AND OURS is so much more rewarding

Don't you know that empathy is the foundation that true sight is born in

That is why TRUE LIFE is about lessons and warnings

The wise live their life as if these signs are extremely important

Whilst fools, all the way through their lives are ignoring

The hidden truths

I've now stopped talking how I'm walking

To those complacent in being dormant

Cus, I now realise that you were always snoring

I no longer waste breath on the deaf

Now, only those seeking will I invest

I'm all about the children and planning and building

But this takes true will

So I refuse to invest my time in those standing still

True Death

You throw your heart out there
But no one's catching
Blood turns to water in a single action
Stomachs churn, when you lose a loved one
Not to the worms
But from their lack of concern
We just got to dust off and keep moving
But only towards those that are showing and proving
Yes, we make mistakes but I hate the saying 'We're only human'
As if that excuses our wrong doing
To overcome we must keep pursuing
We must be of action stemming only from our word
Only then can we distinguish
The purpose of those of true worth
Which is to help and not hurt
Too many won't see sense until their end
And petty judge and condemn
That only brings a false satisfaction
That attempts to justify your own backward actions
That you're masking, we must beware of these distractions
Which are blinding
Due to a self-centredness that stops mankind from seeing the point
In seeking and finding
The doctrine that your sleeping conscience has bound

True Aid

It's in my whole nature to aid

       But you must give according to their stage

            Cus most don't value your sacrifice

                 Most don't realise the true path of life

                     Which is the true path of the wise

Never waste a giving person's time

       It's precious

            To back you, some will go to great measures

The intelligently stupid, foolishly think they have all the answers

But false pride veils the eyes

       That's why you should never be too proud for advice

I realise life is about change and growth

       Whilst fools want yes-men to boost the ego

       My best friend's words cut close to the bone

The key is, that when you give back to the worthy you receive ten-fold

       In other words, when you receive a good act, the more you see

           And put to action, the more you grow

               That fundamentally brings satisfaction to the soul

Love Defined

Too many talk about true love but know not it

       Most think love is how they feel but no, you haven't quite got it

       There are two extremes when love turns dormant

There is absolutely no love in actionless talking

           And absolutely no love in spoiling

It's like when tending to a seed, you drown it by overwatering

True love, it morally and spiritually instructs, it builds up

       Not even the union of man and woman comes before this

       This is called fear, complacency or lust

Loose Lips

Loose lips sink relationships

       Too many are too quick to talk your personal business

              To whom ever has an ear to hear

Even those you hold near and dear, talk causing ill repair

The truth is there can be no love there, from talk mindlessly blared

       But it does make clear those that are fake and those really there

         As the fake make judgements, opinion based

And the real don't judge until everything has been weighed

I live by the commandment, *only talk to aid*

Aid is now based on every sacrifice or decision I make

            Most talk for the sake

The reason for what you say is the foundation of your house

      It's not what goes in your mouth that will truly defile you

      It's what comes out

True Reflections

All praises to the Source for the gifts I've received
From those whose third eye's see the best in me
It's not the material present that I feel, it's the heavy thought
Inspired by the acknowledged presence of the Source that lies behind it
Small thoughtful gifts are like guiding stars, a gift from afar but close
Let me quote the inscription on my bookmark, the same words inscribed in my heart:

God grant me the serenity to accept the things I cannot change
Courage to change the things I can
And the wisdom to know the difference

I put these words above all worldly riches
I give no praise to man, only the one God that moves him
That moves me, how can I take credit for what's beyond me?
      Whom guides me to understanding
And even though I discount nothing, I follow nothing that goes beyond my understanding
      Until I overstand it
           I overstand the fact that the Source guides
               I overstand that once he's no longer recognised
                              You are no longer alive
By forever keeping the source in mind, we are seeking and finding his sacred secrets
      Which is his hidden gift
But everybody wants things in an instance
      So the point of existence is missed
We're fooled by our inner fool into thinking we're saving time
      But we're wasting time, trying to save time
           You can't rush what takes time, like the unravelling of this rhyme
                         Patience is a virtue
                    It takes time to get the truth
But most twist words of truth to defend their backwards views
      I challenge you to remove your veil
           I challenge you to see you're stumbling through hell
           I challenge you because I also fell

-I challenge you because the gift I received urges me to help.

Self (The Keyhole to The Kingdom)

It's not for the creator to convince you
The Source resists fools
To know thy self is to look through the peephole at the naked truth

People want to believe in only what their two eyes see
But that is what the man who leads, uses to deceive
But let us see beneath the surface
Where lies everything's purpose
Our eyes lead us to mathematical workings

If you see a man killed, do your eyes see why?
If you see a plane crash, do your eyes see why?
No, your five senses only aid the reasoning of your mind

Man's true eyes are his understanding
Which is the wisest sight
People don't believe in God, not because their eyes can't see him
But because they can't understand his mathematical reasoning

Every physical thing has a deeper meaning
Can you see the deep connection from a flower to God?
Man has been conned out of making his own decisions
By accepting the information given by a corrupt system
Where men who want to be gods, prefer to keep you lost
Because they fear you being your mentality's boss

So be aware!
They pull the strings of your desires, just so they can fulfil theirs

The Veil

Go running back to your woman's womb

      You're doomed, false goddesses become your seed's tomb

Without submission to the Source, you're submitting to what's been forbidden

      All the desires that man's advocate has hidden

He deceived the disbelievers that he didn't exist

      He deceived those who seek truth outwardly that he was no more than this

         If you can't see within, how can you identify the sin

            A bad seed evolves into a fruitless tree, unless at first, it's seen

He deceived his enemies with pride

      The more knowledge puffs up the ego, the more you die

               Self-inflicted suicide

Outward followers become backward, concentrating on words of truth

            And not truth of words

           And miss the sense

      We shall be judged by our own consciences

      But men, follow men without understanding

I'm inspired to talk in this universal tongue of truth

      All praises to the Source

         All sincere praises given from those who truth stalk

Especially in a time when a once common sense, is now uncommon

         Long forgotten, replaced by a common nonsense

            We truth seekers trod on

Every man has a need to follow

      As every drug addict has a want to fulfil

         There's a pusher on every corner

          There's a truth deformer

Watch out for hooks and spells

      Which can become the basis of your whole outlook

         School yourself before opinionated fools sink their fangs into your innocence

           And infect you with their blindness

Reeled in, now their quest becomes your quest

And you're fighting someone else's war to the death

Seeking righteousness with short sightedness, you get left

Hit by the domino effect of ignorance, now pass it on

Lick by the seven and pride and ego got you putting a veil on

Your wrong

So, a warning must be received from the Source, before his blessings

Only humbleness can lead you to your life's essence

We should always strive to see that we're in the Source's presence

The System

It's time to get unplugged

        Whilst the brain washing box dramatises what's so dramatic

                So the impact of truth becomes surreal

                 Couch potato-heads don't really feel

Peel back the mindless scalp and unreel their tightly coiled film reel

                    Wide open eyed livestock

        Recklessly running to their self-destruction

      To see the obstruction and not do is disgusting

     To those who clearly see and swiftly more

Materialistically clutching

     The material is all you ever craved for, all you claim to know

                Robots with souls

Wasting their gift of life, chasing profit, getting further away from their goal

     To be whole as they fill a hole, hollow

       Ignoring the warnings that always follow

          The only true guidance

Argue with the truth seekers cus you can't bear to listen in the wisdom of deep silence

Battle to the Western life's death

     Battle because your ignorance is bliss

       Battle because you think this life is all you have left

       Battle over material wealth

Do you not understand what it means to be arguing over the worth of something worthless?

     We're all slaves to this system until we truly understand our purpose

It takes one man to change inside and make a change outwardly and raise a nation

Let men change inwardly in their internal fight against Satan

            Man's universal invasion

     That the outwardly distracted claim not to be facing

This isn't the war of the physical

     This is the war of the spiritual, all man's unseen qualities

           Which amounts to aid

            And the aim is to keep qualities intact

-When the clarity of the Source's true maths fades

And the backward mathematics of a Western realm

Tries to overpower your good sense

And take its place

All because man fears knowing beyond what's been given on a plate

So, fears the intimacies of his soul

So, is in a constant state of being afraid

So, is in a constant fear of being spiritually awake

Foundation of the Truth Seekers

You only see as far as your understanding yet you judge that which you don't see
Before you throw stones of words look more closely
Humility is the only key to understanding
Peace is the equilibrium of emotions
Peace is what we must seek or we're moved surfacely
As the surface of the sea

But does what's surface effect what's deep?
That's where the sea's 360 degrees at peace
How can we find the truth if we don't reflect it?
Hypocrites get moved by imbalanced emotions
Which leads to misguided notions
Be as deep and unchanging as the ocean

We have to be in the right condition before we set out to seek
Yes, judge mentals but don't condemn
Only due to your own balance can your analysis be correct
Or else you lose yourself in the depth of your wrong answers
To life's test

Before we seek understanding we must first aim for peace
The foundation of the Truth Seekers

So accept the consequences as life's portion, poor thing
And forget it only stems from your thoughts which leads to actions
So spend your life justifying what's backwards
Blind to the Sources mathematics
Reaping from the foolishness you invested
Now fools prefer to blame God, rather than blame their own perspective

The Purpose of Truth

Without purpose

Words have no truth

Ask yourself, what are your word's use?

Forget the prison rules of grammar

I freely speak and write how I'm inspired to choose

My spoken and written words point's tip is to uplift

I never try clever talk

Yet in riddles truth forever walks

The wise unravel themselves to see truth clear

Whilst fools attempt to unravel the word of truth

Until the word has disappeared

Hidden behind the face of misguided revere

For truth is set in stone

And with freewill man is designed to self-mould

That's why with truth, prophets come

And misunderstood prophets go

Prophets replace each other at every angle that the undeniable truth is disowned

Whilst a lazy people look for one of their own

        To put them on a throne

           So the Christ within themselves remains unknown

Prophets prophesize the gift of truth they've received from the Most High

    For mankind to realise their full potential

        In order for them to seek truth, speak truth and do what's essential

The Employer

The self-centred will do what you allow
It's disgusting how
Self-preservation has these fake ones behaving foul

Good natured employees give a company their all
We live by the rule to always give a little more
But a company that puts business before people
Uses its workers as a crutch as they see themselves as above
They lack the human touch
Cus they're out of touch
As humanity slips out their clutch
And manipulation and exploitation becomes the only way up
It's a selfish path to money and riches
It's nothing personal, it's strictly business
No one dares to challenge their work ethics
So years go by and they don't get the message
That their methods are absolutely pathetic

Who will stand up for the empathetic?
When the jealous are envious of how you graft
And want to have it
But don't have the heart to back it
Because the concept of truly thinking of others, they can't quite grasp it

You're nothing more than a commodity
And no matter how hard you work, when problems arise
The only backing you get is actionless half apologies

My mouth's sword slays evil along with those inactive
Because the price for doing nothing is too massive
They don't want to get involved and ruffle their feathers
So the sloppy's bitchy bully-bwoy tactics are left to fester
So the wise brush off, move on and think whatever

-And hope that these selfish fools are happy together

Foolish Lumps of Clay

With no sense
People caught within moments
Trapped within a chamber that's so tense
Void of past and future, the stale state of chasing tails
Absent of wisdom's tutor
Lustful hearts, caught within a paradox of want
The most cowardly submission giving birth to betrayal

Where's the strength, where's the sense, where's your defence
When you can't defend true principles, you are living a pretence
Living an illusion with the foundation of kidding yourself
Self-contained in a complacency of trying to kid everybody else, you carry the scent of death
In a self-inflicted state of forgetfulness
Only peg by peg, step by step can you pull yourself out of the stench
And begin to self-resurrect

The law of mathematics:
To not know and do is the path of those fake and plastic
But to know and not do is even more backward and tragic
This real-life is harsh on jokers
Stop your rubbishness
With the instant mind frame of hocus pocus

The only way to be released from submitting to eluding moments
Is to stop the rushy-rushy and focus
And realise that the Source guides
And we are part of his grand design
We are entwined with the Most High
If we stop being afraid of change and break stale traits
We'd see, without him we do not control man's way
Don't you know that to follow our lower selves makes us nothing more than…
Foolish lumps of clay

Thoughtlessness

You treat friends like bruders and they act like you're smothering
Now who knows the true meaning of broderine
Too much words and not enough action
Too much brave talk and not enough backing
To back is all about balance and sacrifice
Let's hold back the gun blazing with no fear –
Beware – calm deliberateness cannot be compared
Hot headedness can boil down to thoughtless pride and not thinking clear
Frauds can draw swords in your war
But only your mans-dem is always there

I now can define those weak from those humble
Everybody's living in their bubble
But there's no real wisdom if they're full with thought that talk but don't listen
Becoming their interpretation of their existence
Without truth, there can only be contradiction
If you don't recognise how can you be in recognition?
Truth is not a trend, is not a real-life fiction
It is the only way true men of wisdom can be living

What's the point of good intentions if they remain dormant?
Words that don't materialise should torment
But fools throw out their word as if it's unimportant
The big things can only be reflected by the small ones
The most precious thing the wise can offer is their time
Don't waste it, reciprocate it or become blind to the warning signs
As the Most High sends you right to the back of the line
When it comes to your mans-dem
We must follow these rules as commandments
Keep our morals and laws intact like the 7 locks of Samson
Put no friend above the Most High
By foolishly putting the truth aside
And being more concerned with damaging your friend's pride

Make sure the truth you speak aids and doesn't degrade

There's no point pointing the finger and judging

If it's not encouraging the way, allowing the one who fell from grace to self-elevate

Become more thoughtful of others

And make your internal become one with your external

Making the bubble you live in universal

Where in truth, all reflects one and one reflects all

Because each man cultivating his foundation for the Source draws the same sword

Have empathy for those who truth stalk

Have empathy for those whose lifestyles may contain responsibilities that may differ to yours

Have empathy for those who live a life flawed

But through actions forever fight to evolve

But don't have empathy for those rushy-rushy

Who sacrifice the struggle, the puzzle, for an instant reward

That makes life so ugly

Camouflaged as lovely

The Art of Talking

Holy books aid me in the foundation of my own understanding
But cannot be defined *as* my understanding
My understanding is undeniable thought
          Undeniable talk
             Followed by a definitive walk
    Even though the truth inside guides me to live a life in parallel
      With the way of life, the prophets taught
I still seek until I clearly see
     I never believe truth blindly
        Because in many ways and from the darkest places
                Can the light of truth remind me
      Only what comes out your mouth can defile you and defile others
So, my thoughts swing 360 degrees before I'm talking
        That's the only way to function
         So when the truth is spoken
           There can be no interruptions
The art of talking lies with the true potential of those in discussion
    There can be no thoughtless judging
      Judging the thoughtful without hearing from the judged
   Should be taken as mere eluding assumptions
I heard that it's wrong to cut a man in midst conversation
But I live by the rule that any thoughtlessness in my face deserves instant decapitation

No man should be put above the Most High
No man should claim that he's mathematically aligned at all times
Even the wisest realise that they must continue to strive

To believe - is a condition raised above this worldly system
    Defying all worldly traits with an unsurpassed wisdom
      A 360 degree point of view that leads you to the higher you
It's true, to master the art of talking you must first master the art of listening to the truth

Balls to Backbone

They say this ain't reality
Whilst their thoughts are caught on a physical fantasy
Thoughtless attackers, attack us
They think to perceive and live in our world is madness

How can the distracted distract us?
The true sell-outs, who actually think they're really real
Just cus they're complacent in being actors
When your back-to-front goal is for the 'following masses' to become you master
    Because to aim to please man
        And to reach out for the material hand
           Clutching the physical
      Is a dominant factor
    Of the higher-self detacher

Lifestyles of the rich and famous
    Is the lifestyle of the aimless
When the true reality hits home
    And you don't merely think you know the truth, you simply KNOW
                From BALLS TO BACKBONE
      When the TRUTH goes against all your sticky desires
    And the fear of letting go
      Takes a firm hold
Whilst the proud bully with instantness
    Without empathically explaining a clear path
          But to be on the right track
           Is to look beyond appearances
Is when no man can BOOMIFIE you to submission with his experiences
    When you can listen to every man's opinion without being influenced by your feelings
        But the facts of a spiritual maths
          Also known as your inner compass
           Pointing towards the only path
            That eternally lasts

-Past this physical cast

That's when you're guided by a mathematical intuition

Which is The Mission

As we bring true truth seekers into position

This Lyric is a horn blown to awake born soldiers from a material throne

And alert them to their spiritual posts

Where they're backed by an imperial host

So like dust is blown

So are our inferior foes

We're in war mode

P.C.

Look beyond the stereotypical imagery

A Black man's misery

Where negativity, they subliminally attempt to stick to me

With political wizardry

Unless I wash away my history

And get over it

To be the product of a person

Brutally raped, kidnapped and chained

Whipped and enslaved,

Is close to it

Absolutely sobering

And this infected wound is opening

Address it, or fail miserable

Cus, racists now hide behind a veil of correction political

When Black is connected with what is mindless and physical

Research and embrace cultural truth, put it in the schools

Or undertones of racism will be embedded in the youth

Lab Rats

You're living in a foreign land

    Where you're a minority

        Living in a society where the economy is sovereignty

            And men of colour expect back our heritage

      As though we have leverage

From those who maintain a mind frame devious

    Our addiction to the materialicious

      Has them reading us, preconceiving us

        In order to be subliminally feeding us

          So by our subconscious they can be leading us

                To our graves

              We think we're free

    Cus of the freedom we have to overindulge in materialistic ways

Expect back compensation for 400 years of our bloodline enslaved?

        No, we must rebuild ourselves from a legacy

           Before the chains

Slavery economically paved the way

      Evolving a different type of slave

      With a Western-washed brain

        From slave master to Satan

          From Westernism to Globalisation,

           Infecting every station,

             Having nations self-hating

I don't want your historical biographies, philosophies,

      Or your actionless apologies for your remaining colonies

          ALKE BU LAN man has been dealt with horribly

            All for a foundation built from atrocities

The Israelites

West Indies abandoned like a used tissue

After Europeans misused

Now, nearly 200 years out of slavery

Today's youth, a generation confused

Not taught the truth in schools

Should I feel ashamed that my great great great grandfather was enslaved?

And my African kindred betrayed?

Through human trade?

Now we're looked down the noses of the ignorant of every race

As mankind is betrayed in seven deadly ways

I talk for the seeds but their greed restricts their mind

As they are materialistically inclined,

And as you materialistically climb

Your empathy for others declines

This is the human mathematics that I am inspired to define

The origins of our Caribbean bloodline

In another land, another time

We were the surplus gained in war, famine and for our crimes

The undesirables in an African divide

Traded for guns and liquor

So even more of us could be conquered

And sold to monsters

A 400 year condition

Has us conditioned by a land foreign

For we call it home

At the price of our holy souls

The book of Exodus stated and foretold

That we are the cornerstone

We are so much more than 'exact origin unknown'

Are Your Thoughts Yours?

Are your thoughts yours?
Quiver and shake, question the foundation of your faith
And only with understanding can you discount my inspired words
Or perspective change

Have you been pressured to accept thoughts brought to your door?
The tongue is far deadlier than the sword
Peer pressure gets the better
As we search for birds of our feather

We all have a belief system
      Which is the whole reason we need to believe
                      But the problem is finding the right one
                             But we don't find unless we seek
But through laziness
      We settle for our first answers
            The first place we rest our tiresome feet
                  Deep in complacency
                    The Truth is too tiresome to reach
                Without long-suffering and patience
            We stay unawaken
Fake in an artificial world detached and unrelating
                  To the true education of the purpose of creation
A house can only be as strong as its foundation
      Your foundation is your humbleness
        The bricks are your views
          Without being humble....... you lose
Always be influenced by truth
      By abandoning your weaknesses for your strengths
              Is to remove your pretence
              Which is to define the difference
The impatience of man wants things in his hands when he demands
              That's why he will never understand

-The truth is a sacred secret
Intentionally sealed
Because each man must unravel it before it's revealed
It's the unravelling that's essential

The answers in life are only made to seem instant
In this system of material things which are only meant to represent TRUTH
But man has abused its supreme use for his own use
Which only confuse
So when it comes to our understanding
We give back to Caesar what is to Caesar and to God to God
Which are worlds apart
And we replace this world's artificial light with wise guiding stars
In this self-inflicted dark

The Mathematician

Entered man's world
To get an understanding of science
In the university of mental giants
In order for me to invent for God and that what is in alignment

Those who aid me in my venture
I will always remember

You see, only the Good Samaritan is worthy
I don't respect status, just those who give to the thirsty

True power is mercy

I talk from the heart, unfiltered
This is raw

From amounting to naught and overthrowing life's faults
From life's lessons
This is what I've been taught
It's not whether you live or die
It's how you've walked
To pass on head knowledge brings blessings
But to pass on truth of life's lessons
Is life's blessings
May you be forever in God's presence

As I stumble I witness whom watches me tumble
As they play their game of thrones
Televised drones
Therefore, I walk alone
But along the same pathways and roads
As those
Heading towards God's throne

-Friends are family
People come before a salary
This is my reality

And it's self-preservation that's insanity
                    When put before humanity

I raised myself out of a sticky hell with good decisions
To put people before my selfishness is my religion
This is the truth I'm bringing